ALL AT SEA

Distributed in the United States by
Smart Apple Media
1980 Lookout Drive
North Mankato, MN 56003

Text copyright © Philip Ardagh

Series devised by Philip Ardagh

Philip Ardagh asserts his moral right to be
identified as the author of this work.

ISBN 1-931983-04-6

Library of Congress Control Number: 2002 141313

Printed by South China Printing Co. Ltd., Hong Kong

Editor: Honor Head
Designer: Simeen Karim
Illustrator: Tig Sutton

ALL AT SEA

By Philip Ardagh
Illustrated by Tig Sutton

Thameside Press

It's a busy day at the harbor.

Cars and trucks drive into the back of a ferry.

The bow doors are closed and the ferry sets off to sea.
It passes a hovercraft skimming across the waves.

A crane lowers a
container into the hold
of a cargo ship.

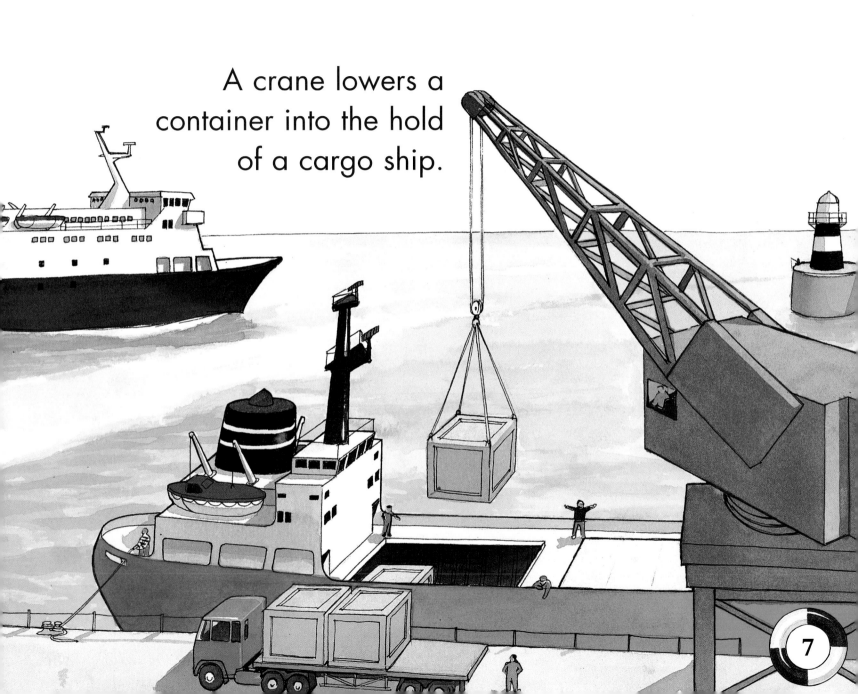

Now the cargo ship is full of containers, it is ready to leave.

Sailors climb aboard their yacht.

9

They hoist the sails
and set off to sea.

The yacht passes a fishing boat
anchored to the seabed.

The fishermen pull in their nets filled with silvery fish.

A speedboat whizzes by.

The speedboat is towing a water-skier behind it.

A periscope appears above the waves.

It's part of a submarine which floats to the surface. A huge ocean liner steams past.

17

The passengers on the ocean liner
wave at an even bigger ship.

It's a huge tanker. Its storage tanks are full of oil.

The tanker is guided into the harbor by tugs.

In the distance, another big ship comes into view.
It's an aircraft carrier.

A helicopter comes in to land
on the deck of the aircraft carrier.

Rows of sailors cheer as an
airplane takes to the skies.

Now all the boats and ships form a convoy. They're all at sea.

Sending off airplanes...

pulling water-skiers fast...

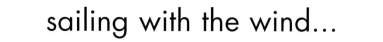

sailing with the wind...

27

waving good-bye!

28

INTERESTING FACTS...

The Nimitz aircraft carrier holds nearly 90 planes and helicopters!

The world's largest ship is an oil tanker. It weighs more than 1,000 jumbo jet airplanes! It's about as long as 4 football fields!

• "Flying fish" don't really fly. They glide over the top of the water. Some stay up over half a minute!

• Ancient Egyptians made boats of "papyrus" reeds. These reeds also made paper!

The world's largest fish is the whale shark. Some are nearly 60 ft long!

Big ocean liners have swimming pools. So you can swim on a ship! On some big passenger ships, you can play golf!

GLOSSARY

aircraft carrier a ship carrying airplanes

anchored held, often with an iron weight in the water

bow doors doors at the front of a ship or boat

container a large box holding a load on a ship

convoy a group moving together, to be safe

ferry a boat taking people and cars across the river or other narrow water

harbor water by land where ships rest

helicopter small aircraft moving straight up with blades

hovercraft a sea craft pushing air below, moving on a "cushion"

periscope a tube with lenses and a mirror; used underwater to see above the water

seabed the floor of the ocean

submarine a ship moving underwater, used mainly in war

tugs small, strong boats that pull ships

INDEX